Donated to the library
In memory of
Kevin Larsen
By
Debra Larsen

Survivor's Science in the
Ocean

Peter D. Riley

Raintree

Chicago, Illinois

© 2005 Raintree
Published by Raintree, a division of Reed Elsevier, Inc.
Chicago, Illinois
Customer Service 888-363-4266
Visit our website at www.raintreelibrary.com

For information, address the publisher:
Raintree, 100 N. LaSalle, Suite 1200, Chicago, IL 60602

Library of Congress Cataloging-in-Publication Data:

Riley, Peter D.
   Survivor's science in the ocean / Peter D. Riley.
      p. cm. -- (Survivor's science)
Summary: Describes the oceans of the world, explains why people go to
sea, and shows what to do to survive in an emergency on the sea.
Includes bibliographical references and index.
   ISBN 1-4109-0229-3 (lib. bdg.)
   1. Oceanography--Juvenile literature. 2. Survival after airplane
accidents, shipwrecks, etc.--Juvenile literature. [1. Oceanography. 2.
Marine ecology. 3. Ecology. 4. Survival.] I. Title. II. Series:
Riley, Peter D. Survivor's science.
   GC21.5.R54 2005
   551.46--dc22

                              2003012728

Printed in Hong Kong.
Bound in the United States.
07 06 05 04 03
10 9 8 7 6 5 4 3 2 1

Acknowledgments
The publisher would like to thank the following for permission to reproduce photographs:
Pp. 4, 30 Norbert Wu/Still Pictures; pp. 6, 7, 28, 34 Stuart Westmorland/Corbis; p. 9 Darrell Gulin/Corbis; p. 12 Gail Mooney/Corbis; p. 13 Yann Arthus-Bertrand/Corbis; p. 14 Jonathan Blair/Corbis; p. 15 Paul A. Souders/Corbis; p. 16 Klaus Andrews/Still Pictures; p. 20 James L. Amos/Corbis; p. 22 (top) Peter Russell, The Military Picture Library/Corbis; p. 22 (bottom) Marques-UNEP/Still Pictures; p. 24 Roland Birke/Still Pictures; p. 26 Yves Lefevre/Still Pictures; p. 29 Brandon D. Cole/Corbis; p. 32 Paul Glendell/Still Pictures; p. 33 Ralph White/Corbis; p. 35 Buddy Mays/Corbis; p. 36 Geoff Tompkinson/Science Photo Library; p. 37 Amos Nauchoum/Corbis; p. 38 Gunther Marx/Corbis; p. 40 Bob Krist/Corbis; p. 42 SETBOUN/Corbis; p. 44 RNLI/PAPicselect; p. 45 Michael Gunther Still Pictures. The science activity photographs and illustrations are by Carole Binding.

Cover photographs: Darrell Gulin/Corbis and Marquez-UNEP/Still Pictures.

Every effort has been made to contact copyright holders of any material reproduced in this book. Any omissions will be rectified in subsequent printings if notice is given to the publisher.

Content Consultant:
Karen Carney is a graduate student in Learning Science at Northwestern University. Prior to this she was an Earth Science and Geology teacher at Collegiate School in New York City. Karen has worked as a geological field and lab researcher, specializing in fossil preservation and sedimentary environments.

Some words are shown in bold, **like this.** You can find out what they mean by looking in the glossary.

Contents

Introduction

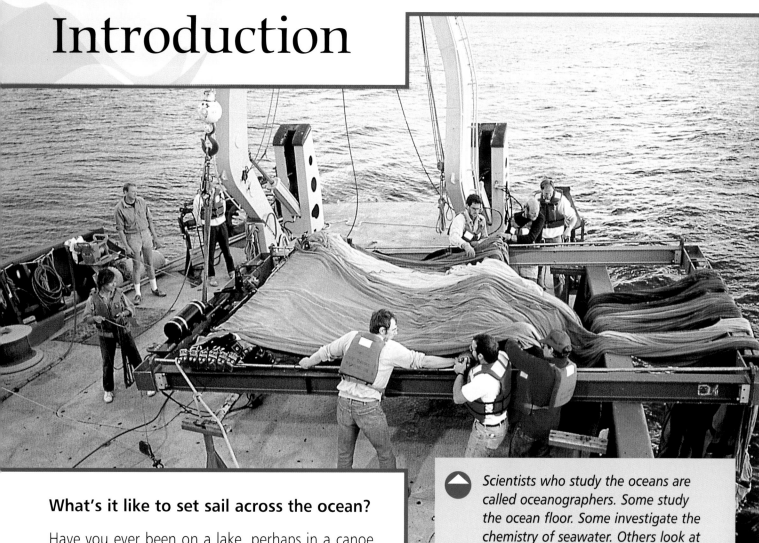

What's it like to set sail across the ocean?

Have you ever been on a lake, perhaps in a canoe or row boat? The water was probably calm and the shore was never far away. Now imagine setting sail across the ocean. You step on board your boat, ready to leave the harbor. The engine roars, the propeller turns, and off you go. Soon the land disappears from view and all you can see in the distance is water.

The keys to survival

People have sailed on the seas and oceans for thousands of years. The first reason for sailing was probably to catch fish. Later, people used boats to explore along the coasts. Eventually some people, such as the Polynesians and the Vikings, crossed the water to settle in distant lands. Today many

Scientists who study the oceans are called oceanographers. Some study the ocean floor. Some investigate the chemistry of seawater. Others look at currents, waves, and tides, and some study ocean plants and animals.

people work on boats, including fishing boats, oil tankers, cargo ships, and cruise ships. Some people make expeditions across the oceans and seas to study marine wildlife, search for resources, or make discoveries about how the ocean currents flow.

More than two-thirds of the earth is covered by water. We are going to see how people have learned to survive journeys across the oceans, and look at some of the many living things that inhabit these vast, watery places.

Discovering with science

For thousands of years people have investigated their surroundings and made discoveries that have helped them survive. About 400 years ago a way of investigating called the scientific method was devised to help us understand our world more clearly. The main features of the scientific method are:

1 Making an **observation**

2 Thinking of an idea to explain the observation

3 Doing a test or experiment to test the idea

4 Looking at the result of the test and comparing it with the idea

Today the scientific method is used to provide explanations for almost everything. In this book you can try some science activities and find out about the science that helps people traveling across the oceans and exploring marine life to understand the conditions and the creatures they might meet. In the activities you may use the entire scientific method or just parts of it, such as making observations or doing experiments. But you will always be using science to make discoveries.

Are you ready to find out how people survive at sea? Turn the page to find out about the oceans and seas of the world.

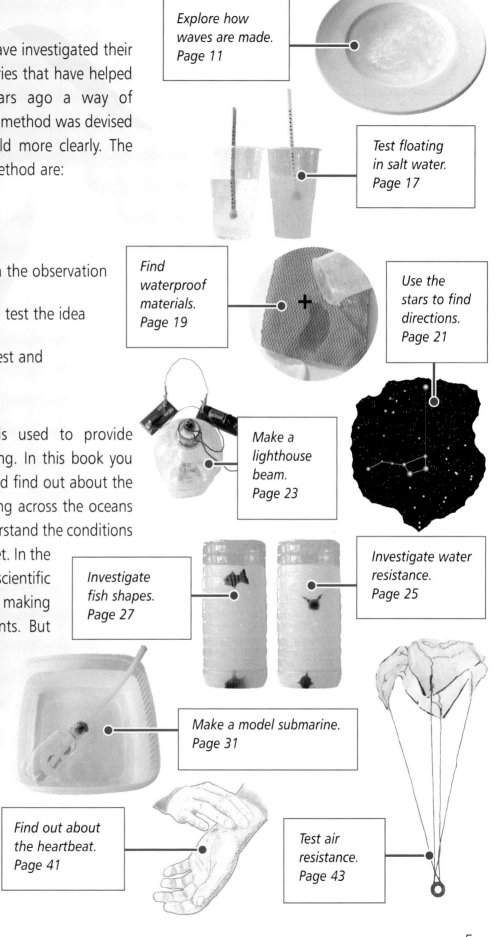

Explore how waves are made. Page 11

Test floating in salt water. Page 17

Find waterproof materials. Page 19

Use the stars to find directions. Page 21

Make a lighthouse beam. Page 23

Investigate water resistance. Page 25

Investigate fish shapes. Page 27

Make a model submarine. Page 31

Find out about the heartbeat. Page 41

Test air resistance. Page 43

Oceans and Seas of the World

Just over two-thirds of the earth's surface is covered by saltwater. The largest areas of this water, between the continents, are called oceans. Areas of saltwater closer to the land, or partly or completely surrounded by land, are called seas.

The Pacific, the Atlantic, and the Indian Oceans are so large that each is divided into two parts—that in the Northern Hemisphere and that in the Southern Hemisphere.

You may have heard the saying "to sail the seven seas." It comes from past times, when sailors said there were seven oceans: the North and South Atlantic, the North and South Pacific, the North and South Indian Ocean, and the Arctic Ocean. (Parts of what they called the South Atlantic, the South Pacific and the South Indian Ocean make up what we call the Antarctic Ocean today.)

Arctic Ocean

North America

Atlantic Ocean

Tropic of Cancer

Caribbean Sea

Equator

Pacific Ocean

South America

Tropic of Capricorn

People on the oceans and seas

It would be possible to spend your whole life at sea, provided that you visited land occasionally to stock up on food and drinking water. However, people don't live like this. They may visit the water for a few hours, days, or months, to catch fish, to vacation, or to transport oil and other goods between countries. Some people spend time on the water living on oil rigs, which are anchored to the ocean floor. Oceans and seas are also used for sport, and there are sometimes yacht races across oceans or seas around the world.

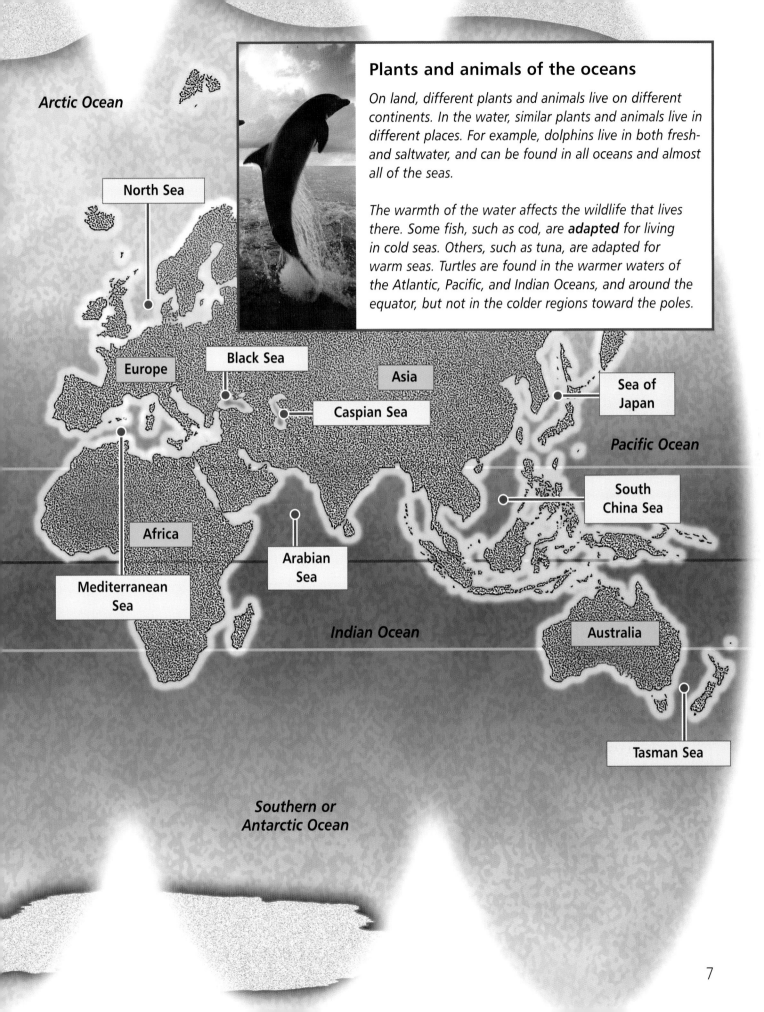

Arctic Ocean

North Sea

Plants and animals of the oceans

On land, different plants and animals live on different continents. In the water, similar plants and animals live in different places. For example, dolphins live in both fresh- and saltwater, and can be found in all oceans and almost all of the seas.

The warmth of the water affects the wildlife that lives there. Some fish, such as cod, are **adapted** for living in cold seas. Others, such as tuna, are adapted for warm seas. Turtles are found in the warmer waters of the Atlantic, Pacific, and Indian Oceans, and around the equator, but not in the colder regions toward the poles.

Europe

Black Sea

Asia

Caspian Sea

Sea of Japan

Pacific Ocean

South China Sea

Africa

Arabian Sea

Mediterranean Sea

Indian Ocean

Australia

Tasman Sea

Southern or Antarctic Ocean

Ocean Currents

The water in the oceans is never still. Winds blow on the surface, creating currents in the upper layer of the water. In most oceans, these currents move in circular paths called **gyres.**

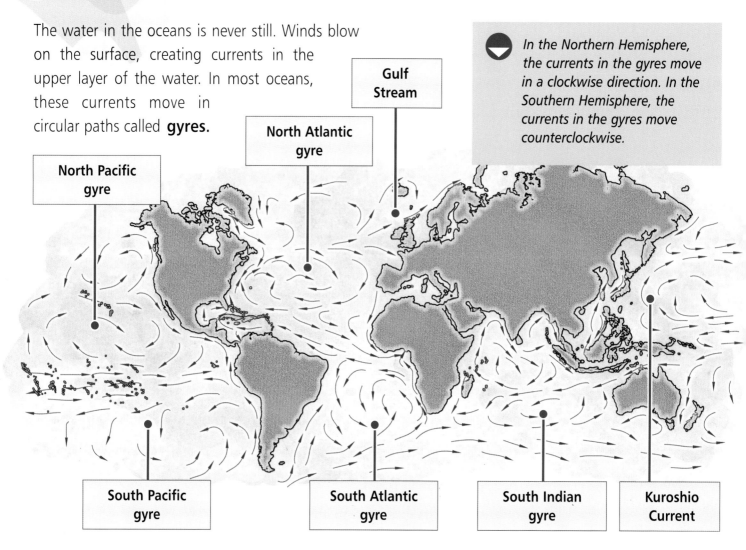

In the Northern Hemisphere, the currents in the gyres move in a clockwise direction. In the Southern Hemisphere, the currents in the gyres move counterclockwise.

Gulf Stream

North Atlantic gyre

North Pacific gyre

South Pacific gyre

South Atlantic gyre

South Indian gyre

Kuroshio Current

Prevailing winds are air currents in different parts of the world that constantly blow in one direction. In the Northern Hemisphere, the Northeast trade winds blow the water to the west, and the Westerlies blow the water to the east. These winds create the currents in the North Atlantic gyre and the North Pacific gyre.

In the Southern Hemisphere, the Southeast trade winds and westerly winds known as the Roaring Forties create the currents in the gyres in the South Pacific, South Atlantic, and South Indian Oceans. The speed of most ocean currents is about 6 miles (10 kilometers) a day.

Warm and cool currents

The Sun's rays heat the earth most intensely at the equator. So the water in the oceans at the equator is warmer than water to the north and south. Currents flowing from the equator are currents of warm water. Those near the poles carry cooler water.

How the earth's spin affects the currents

The revolution of the earth affects the water currents. If you look down on the north pole of a globe and turn it counterclockwise, you are making it revolve to the east like the earth does. As the earth turns eastward, the North Atlantic and North Pacific waters gather in large amounts on the oceans' western sides. This large amount of water pushes strongly on the water to the north of it, causing the currents traveling north to move at speeds of 60–100 miles (100–160 kilometers) a day.

In the North Atlantic, this fast-moving current is called the Gulf Stream. In the North Pacific, the fast-moving current is called the Kuroshio Current. Both currents are also helped on their way by the wind.

Current complications and dangers

Other things that affect the way ocean currents move include the temperature of the water and the amount of salt it contains. The movement of the currents is very complicated. They don't just move across the surface of the water, but up and down in the oceans, too.

While ocean currents can help people sail along, they can also cause great danger. Where two ocean currents meet, they can crash into each other, causing large waves.

 This large wave has been made where two ocean currents meet. These currents flow off the coast of Oregon (see diagram on page 8).

How Are Waves Made?

Most waves on an ocean or sea are made by the wind. The size of the wave depends on three things: the distance the wind blows across the water (this is called the fetch), the length of time the wind blows, and the speed of the wind.

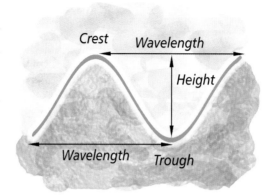

Crest · Wavelength · Height · Wavelength · Trough

Every wave has a **crest** and a **trough**. The height of a wave is measured from its trough to its crest. Wavelength is the distance between two crests or two troughs.

Ripples

How the wind pushes on waves

Windward side · Leeward side

How a wave builds up

A very gentle wind makes small waves called ripples, with rounded crests. The ripples stay rounded and smooth because forces between molecules of the water produce **surface tension,** which makes the water surface seem to have a thin skin.

As the wind increases, it pushes the crests farther apart and makes the wavelength longer. Now gravity becomes more important in shaping the wave, pulling down the water between the crests. There are two sides to a wave crest—the windward side, where the air pushes with a strong force, and the leeward side, where the air pushes with less force. This difference in the way the air pushes on the wave crest makes the crest even more pointed.

When the sides of the crest make an angle of 120 degrees with each other, surface tension can no longer hold the water surface on the crest like a skin and it breaks up. When this happens, the crest forms a whitecap. A sea with white wave crests can be a danger to a small boat because the waves may turn the boat over.

When a wave breaks

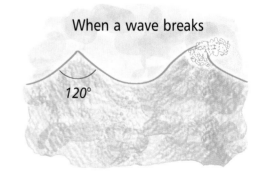

120°

Make a storm in a soup bowl

You can make **observations** on waves by creating some yourself in a soup bowl full of water.

You need a soup bowl with a broad rim, water, paper and pencil. + + +

1 Fill the bowl with water and put it near the edge of the table.

2 Sit down so that you can bring your mouth close to the rim of the bowl.

3 Blow gently on the water and look at the pattern of waves. Look for the way they cast shadows on the bottom of the bowl.

4 Draw the pattern you have seen.

5 Blow again more strongly, then draw the pattern.

6 Try blowing for different lengths of time, then draw the patterns.

7 When the water has settled, make a large number of very short, very strong blows. This should cause a chaotic wave pattern that may splash over the rim of the bowl!

Sketch the pattern you see in the water.

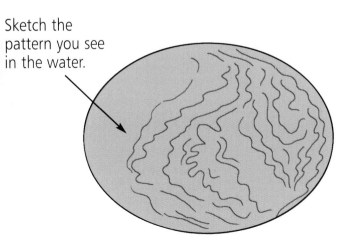

Waves on the beach

Often the wind makes waves with a low **crest** and a very long wavelength. They move across the water, making the surface rise and fall as they go. This movement of the surface is called a **swell.**

When the waves in a swell reach the shallow water of a beach, their wavelength becomes shorter and their height increases. If the slope of the beach is gentle, the wave crests rise and break gradually to form **foam.** If the slope of the beach is steep, the wave crests rise quickly and the wave tips over and plunges down, making large amounts of **spray.**

How waves may break on a gently sloping beach

How waves break on a steep beach

Gently sloping beach

Steeply sloping beach

Freak waves and tsunamis

Freak waves sometimes occur in storms. In a storm, wind pushes on the water surface and makes waves with high crests and deep troughs. If the waves are made against the flow of a strong current like the Gulf Stream, more water is pushed into them and they rise even higher. Freak waves may reach a height of 80–100 feet (24–30 meters), large enough to sink a supertanker.

Another kind of huge wave happens when an earthquake occurs or a volcano erupts under the sea. It is called a tsunami. Out on the ocean, a tsunami may be less than 3 feet (1 meter) high, but as it moves toward land it becomes a wall of water over 100 feet (30 meters) high.

 It is safer to launch and land a boat on a gently sloping beach, because the waves tend to be smaller.

Safe harbors

Since the wind plays a large part in making waves, places that are sheltered from the wind have smaller waves and make safer places to launch and land boats. Harbors are built in more sheltered places along a coast.

Tides

The **tides** are the movement of the ocean up and down the shore. They are caused by the pull of gravity of the Moon and the Sun on the water in the oceans. The Moon's pull of gravity tugs the ocean water into a bulge where the earth is closest to the Moon. On the other side of the earth, a similar bulge of water develops.

Every day, as the earth rotates, the bulge of water affects different parts of the coastline, causing the tide to rise up the shore. As that part of the coastline moves away from the position where the bulge occurs, the tide moves back down the beach.

Twice a month, as the Moon goes around the earth, the Sun's gravity pulls on the earth's water in line with the Moon's gravity. This makes the tides rise higher and fall lower than at other times.

Currents near the shore

When the tide moves toward the shore, water can rush between islands and **sandbars,** making strong currents. Similar currents occur in the opposite direction as the tide moves away from the shore. These currents can push a boat or ship onto a sandbar, or dash it against rocks and sink it.

How the Moon's gravity causes tides

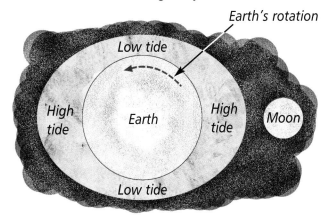

How the Sun's gravity affects tides

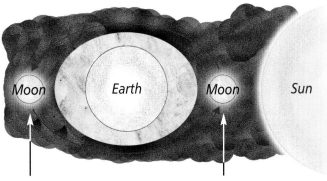

Twice a month the Sun, Moon, and Earth are aligned and the tides are at their greatest.

Tides can produce strong currents where there are islands and sandbars.

How Boats Float

When a boat is on the beach, its weight pushes down on the ground. Once the boat has been pushed into the water, another force acts on it. This force is called **buoyancy.** It is due to the push of the water, but where does the push come from?

Boats are very heavy. Do you wonder why they float?

When an object is placed in water, it pushes some of the water out of the way. You can easily see this happen if you fill a cup to the brim with water, place it in a saucer, and put an apple in the water. The apple floats in the water but pushes out some water so that it can get in. This water spills over into the saucer.

If you weigh the apple and then weigh the water in the saucer, you will find that both weigh the same. Since weight is a force and buoyancy is a force, this means that the force of the buoyancy pushing up is the same as the force of the weight pushing down. This balance of forces makes the apple float.

An apple floats in a cup of water. The water it pushes out of the cup weighs the same as the apple.

Any object that floats, such as a boat or a ship, has buoyancy pushing up on it that is the same as its weight or greater than its weight.

If an object sinks, its weight is greater than the buoyancy pushing on it. If you repeat the experiment with the apple, cup, and saucer, but replace the apple with a ball of modeling clay, you get a different result. The ball sinks. The weight of the ball is much greater than the weight of water it displaces.

However, if the same piece of modeling clay is reshaped to make a hollow boat-shaped object, it floats. The new shape has a larger area in contact with the water, and so it pushes more water away. But its weight has not increased very much because the hollow is only filled with air. The weight of the air and the modeling clay in the boat is less than the buoyancy, and so the boat floats.

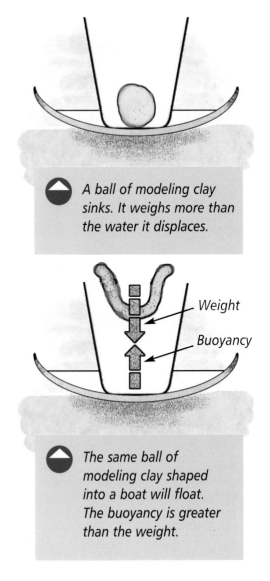

A ball of modeling clay sinks. It weighs more than the water it displaces.

Weight

Buoyancy

The same ball of modeling clay shaped into a boat will float. The buoyancy is greater than the weight.

If you could repeat this experiment with steel, you would get the same result. Steel boats float because the weight of the steel and the air inside the boat is less than the buoyancy.

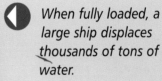

When fully loaded, a large ship displaces thousands of tons of water.

Floating Around the World

A ship sails out of port in Hamburg, Germany, along the Elbe River into the North Sea.

All substances such as air, water, and rock are made of tiny particles that can only be seen with powerful microscopes. In air and other gases, the particles are free to move around. In water and other liquids, the particles stay close together and slide over each other. In rocks and other solids, the particles are locked together. This concept of particles helps to explain what happens when a boat floats around the world.

Imagine that a boat starts its journey on a river in Northern Europe. In this cold water the particles come very close together. Each particle pushes on the boat and together they make a strong force, so that the boat floats high in the water.

When the boat enters the ocean or sea, it floats even higher. Particles of salt in the seawater have added their pushing force to that of the water particles.

As the boat travels south and into the **Tropics**, the water becomes warmer and warmer. The particles in warmer water are more spread out and so they push with less force on the boat and it floats lower in the water.

Finally the boat sails into a river in a tropical country. The water is warm but does not contain salt to give an extra push. The boat floats even lower.

An overloaded boat is in danger of sinking if caught in a storm. In the 1800s Samuel Plimsoll introduced a way of knowing whether a boat was safely loaded. Plimsoll lines, drawn on the side of a boat, show the safe levels for the boat to float in different kinds of water.

Plimsoll lines

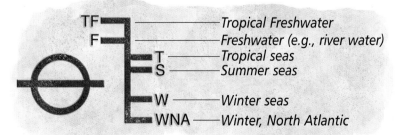

TF — Tropical Freshwater
F — Freshwater (e.g., river water)
T — Tropical seas
S — Summer seas
W — Winter seas
WNA — Winter, North Atlantic

Do things float higher in saltwater?

When scientists review information, they sometimes carry out experiments to check if it is correct. Use this experiment to check the information on page 16.

You need water, a graduated cylinder or measuring cup, two clear plastic cups, spoon, salt, two plastic straws, marker, modeling clay.

1 Pour exactly the same amount of water into each cup, so they are both about two-thirds full.

2 Add salt, a spoonful at a time, to the water in one cup until no more will dissolve. You can tell this has happened because salt crystals will stay undissolved at the bottom of the cup.

3 Make scales on the straws by putting marks on them at quarter-inch (half-centimeter) intervals.

4 Make two identical pieces of modeling clay and fix one to each straw. Check that the straws float upright in the water without salt.

5 Move one straw to the saltwater and look at the scale on each straw. Does the water level come to the same mark on each scale?

Clothes for Sailing

The body needs to keep warm at all times. For people sailing in tropical seas, the weather may be so warm that only shorts and t-shirts are needed. Any exposed skin must be coated with **sunblock,** to stop the Sun's **ultraviolet** rays from damaging the skin. In cooler waters, thicker clothes should be worn to keep in the body heat.

Wet-weather clothes

If only light showers are expected, coats or jackets made from water-repellent material may be enough to keep you dry. These materials are made from fibers coated in chemicals called silicones. They make water drops bead up and slide off the material. Gaps between the fibers let out water vapor in sweat, to keep the body comfortable. These materials are widely used for jackets and windbreakers.

In a storm, heavy rain and waves would push water through the gaps between the fibers of water-repellent clothing and you would be soaked. Instead, you need clothes made from waterproof material. Its fibers are coated with substances such as oil, rubber, or a plastic material that block the air spaces between them.

Fluorescent patches on the hood glow when light shines on them. They help rescuers find shipwrecked people at night.

A strobe light sends out flashes of light to show where the person is.

A whistle can be used in the fog.

A flare gun is used to send a bright flare high into the sky to attract attention.

A life jacket inflates to keep the wearer afloat.

The high collar, adjustable cuffs, and ankle fasteners keep out water.

 Waterproof clothing for stormy waters is called foul-weather gear. Since there is also a danger of shipwreck in a storm, the foul-weather gear includes equipment and materials to help people who need to be rescued.

Which material is waterproof?

1 Look at the materials and guess which will stop water from passing through.

2 Cut a square from each type of material. All the squares should be the same size.

3 Cut squares of paper towel slightly smaller than the squares of material. Make sure the paper towel squares are all the same size.

4 Put a square of material over a square of paper towel. Measure a small amount of water into the graduated cylinder, then pour it onto the material.

5 After 2 minutes, remove the material and examine the paper towel. Is it wet?

6 Repeat steps 4 and 5 with the other materials.

7 Divide the pieces of material into a waterproof group and a nonwaterproof group.

8 Which materials could be used for making waterproof clothes?

*You could continue your investigation by considering that waterproof clothes also need to be **flexible**. Test each material that you found to be waterproof by bending and unbending it a number of times and then checking to see if this has made it less waterproof.*

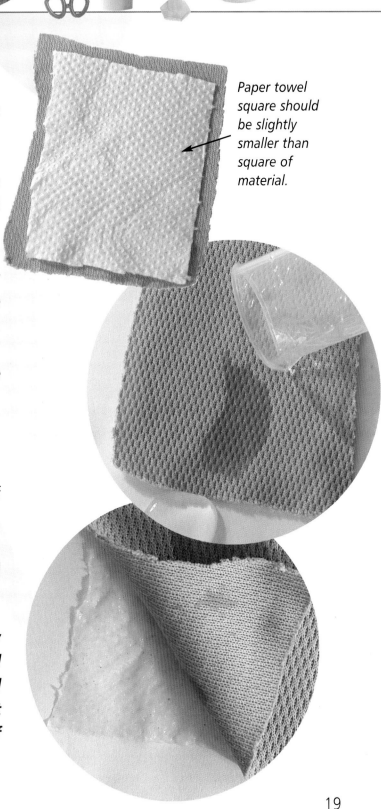

Paper towel square should be slightly smaller than square of material.

19

Finding a Way

The first people to sail the oceans and seas used many **observations** to guide them. They observed the direction of the wind, the direction of the currents, the patterns of the waves, the saltiness of the water, the types of clouds in the sky, and the directions that the birds flew.

Wherever sailors went, they recorded the positions of features on coasts, the depth of the water, and the occurrence of **sandbars** and low tide. All this information was used to make maps, which are carried on board all kinds of ships and boats today.

Stick charts

Native sailors in the South Pacific made maps called stick charts, using shells and lengths of cane. The shells showed the positions of islands, and the pieces of cane showed the currents. Sailors memorized the stick chart before they set sail.

The compass and sextant

A map is only useful if the sailors know their position. A compass helps them to find the direction they are sailing, but their exact position in the water is more difficult to calculate.

In clear weather, a sextant can be used to measure the height of the Sun above the horizon. By looking in special tables for this measurement and the time it was taken, sailors can find the position of the ship. The sextant can be used when land cannot be seen, and so its invention enabled sailors to explore farther out across the waters.

 *A sextant has a mirror and an eyeglass, with a light **filter** to protect the eye. The sailor moves the mirror along the sextant arm until it reflects the Sun onto his view of the horizon. A scale on the sextant arm gives the height of the Sun.*

Use the stars to find north and south

At night, the positions of the stars can help sailors find the direction in which they are sailing.

You need a clear view of the night sky (preferably away from streetlights) and an adult to accompany you.

In the Northern Hemisphere

1 Look into the sky and find the constellation called the Big Dipper. You can also think of it as a saucepan.

2 Look for the two stars farthest from the "pan handle" (Think of them as A and B.)

3 In your mind, measure the distance between A and B.

4 In your mind, make a line from A and B out into space. The line should be about five times the distance between A and B. At this point you should find a star called the North Star (or polestar). It is in the direction of north.

In the Southern Hemisphere

1 Look into the sky and find the constellation called the Southern Cross.

2 In your mind, measure the length of the longest part of the cross.

3 In your mind, extend a line from the bottom of the cross into space. Make this line about four and half times the length of the long part of the cross. Look down to the horizon at this point and you will be looking south.

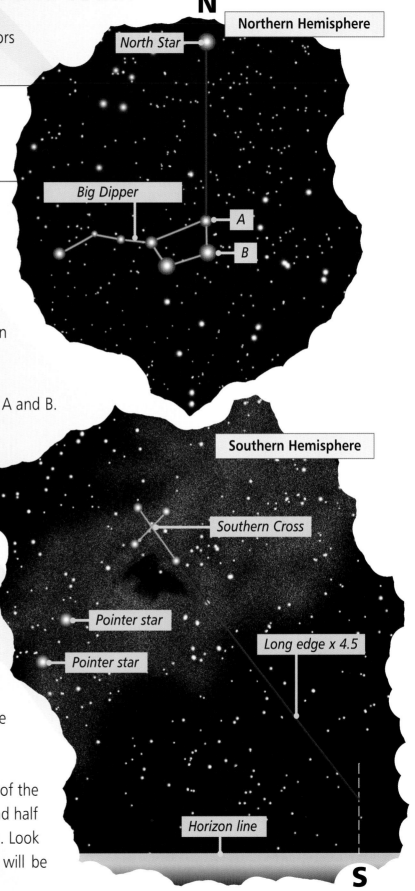

N

Northern Hemisphere

North Star

Big Dipper

A

B

Southern Hemisphere

Southern Cross

Pointer star

Long edge x 4.5

Pointer star

Horizon line

S

21

GPS

GPS stands for global positioning system. It is a system of **satellites** that allows you to find your position anywhere, on land or sea. There are many satellites in orbit around the earth, including 24 that constantly send out signals about their position.

A person using GPS carries a receiver about the size of a mobile phone. When it is switched on, it searches for signals from four of the 24 satellites. The signals are sent into a computer in the receiver, and the position of the person is shown on a screen. This can then be used with a map to help plot the journey.

GPS is widely used by ships and boats, but it can break down. It is then that older methods of finding a way, such as using a sextant or looking at the stars, have to be used.

A GPS receiver is a useful tool for people on an expedition.

Lighthouses are not just useful at night. They are painted so that they stand out from their surroundings and can be easily seen in daylight, too.

Coastal waters

On the ocean, sailors must battle with currents and winds to stay on course. Near the coast, they must be careful not to run their ships onto rocks just below the water surface. Many hazards near the coast are marked with **buoys** that float on the water above them.

At night the outline of the coast is difficult to see. On many coasts lighthouses show sailors where the coast is and also help them find their position on a map. Each lighthouse sends out a distinct beam of light for a certain length of time, as marked on the sailors' maps. This allows sailors to identify which lighthouse they are near.

Make a beam from a lighthouse

The lamp in a lighthouse stays on all through the night. A group of **lenses** turn around it to send out a beam. A lens is not used in the simple design here. However, you may like to improve the design and use a magnifying glass.

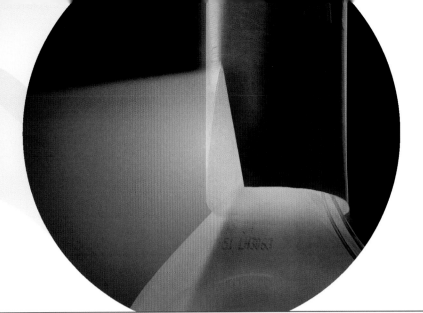

You need a 1.5V battery, a switch, a 3V bulb, three wires with clips, a plastic bottle, tape, a piece of stiff black paper.

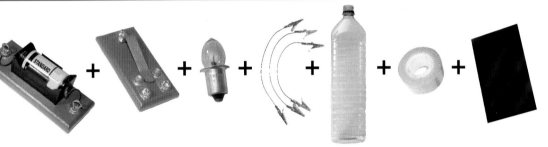

Warning!

To avoid blowing out the bulb, make sure it has the same or a higher voltage than the battery.

1 Make an electric circuit as shown in the photograph, with the bulb taped to the top of the bottle.

2 Make a cover with a slit in it out of the black paper, to fit over the top of the "lighthouse."

3 Darken the room and switch on the light in the lighthouse. Turn the top of the lighthouse. Can you make a beam sweep around the room?

Run one wire from the positive end of the battery to the "on" side of the switch.

Run a second wire from the negative end of the battery to the base of the bulb.

Attach the paper cover with slit.

Run the third wire from the switch to the base of the bulb.

Tape the bulb to the top of the bottle.

The Key to Life in the Ocean

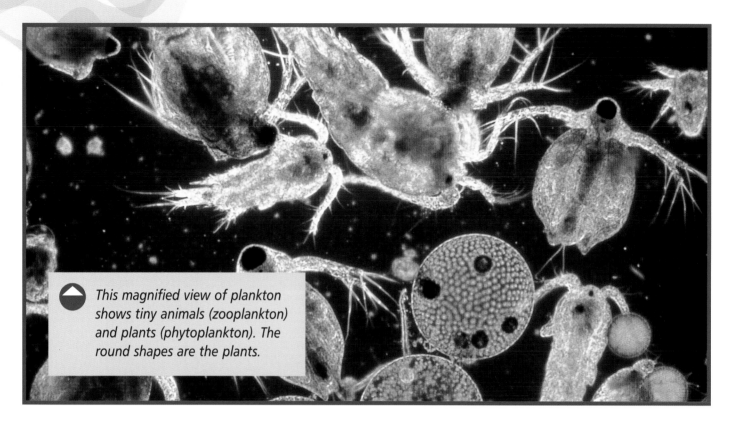

This magnified view of plankton shows tiny animals (zooplankton) and plants (phytoplankton). The round shapes are the plants.

Plankton is formed from huge numbers of very tiny plants and animals. They form a great cloud of microscopic life that lies just below the surface of all oceans and seas.

The plants in the plankton

The microscopic plants are called **algae.** They have tiny bodies. Many are made from just one **cell,** and others are made from groups of cells. Inside each plant is a green **pigment** called chlorophyll. It traps energy from sunlight, and the plant uses this energy to make food.

As rays of sunlight shine down through the water, they lose their energy and become dimmer as they go deeper. The plants need bright light to make food, and so they must stay near the water surface.

Some algae have drops of oil in them to help them float. Others have spikes that help slow the plant as it sinks. The spikes also catch upward-moving currents to bring the plant back to the surface.

Animals in the plankton

Huge numbers of tiny animals feed on the algae. Many are shrimplike animals called copepods, but there are young crabs, lobsters, and starfish, too. The plankton is a nursery for many small animals and many fish lay their eggs there. The tiny animals are eaten by larger animals, such as comb jellies and small fish. These are eaten by larger fish that may then be eaten by dolphins or other top predators. The way the animals are linked together through feeding is called a food chain. Algae is the foundation of the food chain for all animals in the ocean.

Investigating spikes

You can investigate the effect of spikes on sinking by letting model algae fall through a thick liquid made with wallpaper paste. The models sink more slowly in this than they would in water, so it is easier to compare their sinking speeds. The force that slows the sinking speed is called water resistance. It depends on the shape of the sinking body.

You need wallpaper paste (nonallergenic), a tall plastic bottle, scissors, modeling clay, stopwatch.

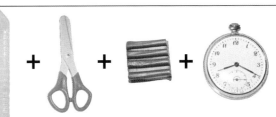

1 Ask an adult to mix the wallpaper paste. It should be somewhat clear yet fairly thick. Also ask the adult to cut the neck off the plastic bottle.

2 Pour the thick liquid into the bottle.

3 Divide the modeling clay into several balls, all the same size. Leave one ball alone but make models of spiky algae with the others. Make one model with two spikes, one with three spikes, and so on.

4 Predict which model will sink the fastest and which will sink the slowest.

5 Drop each model in, one at a time, and time its fall if possible. If the models fall too quickly, make models from smaller pieces of modeling clay and try again.

6 Compare your results with your predictions.

Time the fall of each model.

25

Moving Quickly in Water

If you try to walk through water in a swimming pool, you will find it slow and tiring. When you swim, you move much more quickly and easily. Many fish swim much faster than we do, to catch food and avoid **predators.** Their spindle shape allows the water to flow smoothly over their body so they can travel quickly.

Most of a fish's body is packed with **muscle,** to move its sides and its tail back and forth. This movement of body and tail pushes the fish through the water. This is a much more efficient way of swimming than using arms and legs as we do.

When people swim, they have to turn their head occasionally to bring their mouth and nose out of the

Spindle-shaped fish

Pancake-shaped fish

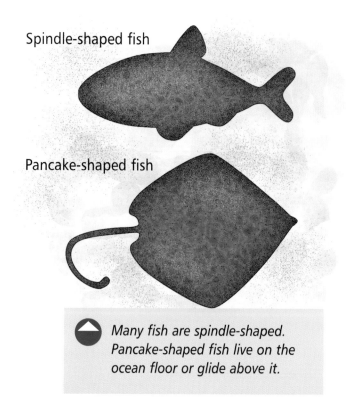

Many fish are spindle-shaped. Pancake-shaped fish live on the ocean floor or glide above it.

The side-to-side movement of a shark's tail makes it swim quickly through the water.

water so that they can breathe. A fish does not have this problem because it has **gills** inside its head. Gills allow it to breathe underwater by taking **oxygen** from the water and giving out **carbon dioxide.**

Moving up and down

A person has to swim hard to go deeper in the water, but many fish can rise and sink in the water without using the muscles in their tail and sides. They have an organ in their body called the swim bladder, which holds a gas released from the blood. When the fish wants to sink, it takes gas back into the blood and the swim bladder shrinks. This makes the fish less **buoyant** and it sinks.

When the fish wants to rise in the water, it releases more gas into its swim bladder. This makes the fish more buoyant and it rises in the water.

Investigating fish shapes

Sometimes scientists use the same equipment to make two or more investigations. In this activity you use the same materials as on page 25, but this time to investigate how shape affects the speed at which an object moves. Some fish are spindle-shaped and some are pancake-shaped. Which shape do you think would help a fish move faster? Try this investigation to find out if you are right.

You need wallpaper paste (nonallergenic), a tall plastic bottle, scissors, modeling clay, stopwatch.

1 Follow instructions 1 and 2 on page 25.

2 Divide the modeling clay into three equal-sized balls. Leave one alone but use the others to make models of fish, one with a spindle shape and one with a pancake shape.

3 Predict which of the three models will sink the fastest and which the slowest.

4 Drop each in turn into the liquid and time its fall if possible. If the models fall too quickly, make smaller ones and try again.

5 Make model fish shapes using your own ideas and compare their speeds.

Time the fall of each model.

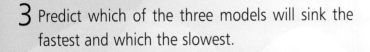

Dolphins and Whales

Dolphins often accompany a boat or ship as it sails along. They swim near the bow (front) and at the sides of the vessel and sometimes playfully leap out of the water. Occasionally the crew may be lucky enough to see a whale swimming by. Dolphins and whales are **adapted** for life in water, but must return to the surface to breathe air.

Fishlike mammals

Dolphins and whales are sometimes described as fish, because they have the spindle shape of a fish. This is incorrect. Dolphins and whales are **mammals,** like us, and this gives them two problems that fish do not have. All mammals obtain the oxygen they need from air, and have **lungs** to let them do this. They must also keep their bodies warm. By contrast, fish have gills to obtain their oxygen from water. Their body temperature can change with the temperature of the water without harm.

Regularly throughout the day and night, whales and dolphins must return to the water surface to breathe. They have nostrils on the top of their heads. This allows them

 Dolphins have a long, slender snout and a streamlined body. This allows them to move smoothly through the water.

to float at the water surface as they breathe, and not to have to rise out of the water. When the whale or dolphin dives again, its nostrils close to keep water out of its **airways.**

The skin of whales and dolphins has a layer beneath the surface that is filled with fat and oil. This material is called blubber. It is a layer of **insulation.** This means that it acts like a blanket, keeping heat inside the body from passing to the water. Without its layer of blubber, a whale or dolphin would soon die in cold waters.

How they feed

All dolphins and some whales, such as the sperm whale and killer whale, have teeth. They use their teeth and jaws to grab and hold prey, but do not use them for chewing.

Some whales do not have teeth. They have large flaps that hang down from their upper jaw like curtains. The flaps are called **baleen** and the whales that have them are called baleen whales. The humpback whale and the blue whale are two examples.

Bristles on the edges of the baleen plates make a **filter.** The whale takes a large amount of water into its mouth. This water may contain the whale's food of shrimp or fish. The whale then raises its tongue and forces the water out through the bristles. This leaves the food trapped on the inside of the mouth, ready to be swallowed.

A humpback whale opens its mouth to feed. Humpback whales are found worldwide.

Going Deeper

Before you dive, you breathe in deeply to take as much air into your **lungs** as possible. During the dive, you use up the **oxygen** in the air in your lungs to release energy, so that your arms and legs can move to swim. Since people are **mammals,** and cannot breathe underwater, you must return to the water surface to take your next breath. If you wanted to stay underwater a long time, you would need to carry a tank of **compressed air** on your back to breathe as you were swimming along.

Submarines

In 1620 Cornelius Drebbel invented a craft that could take people underwater. It had leather bags filled with water to make the craft sink. To make it rise, the bags were filled with air. This craft was the first submarine. By the end of the 1800s, people discovered ways to make submarines move along through the water. They used **diesel** engines for moving at the surface, and battery-powered motors for traveling underwater. Submarines are very large craft, used mainly in the navy but sometimes in exploration.

Submersibles

Smaller underwater craft called **submersibles** are used for many kinds of exploration, such as searching for new kinds of life in the deep oceans, investigating the rocks on the ocean floor, and examining shipwrecks.

Pressure

As an underwater craft makes a dive, the pressure of the water around it increases. This is because of the weight of water pushing down from above. Air inside the craft for the crew to breathe pushes outward on the walls of the craft, but with much less pressure than the water pushing inward. If the walls of the craft were weak, the whole craft would soon collapse inward. All deep-sea craft must have strong walls to withstand the pressure of the water.

Submersibles can take scientists right down to the ocean floor.

Make a model submarine

Submarines have spaces in them called **ballast** tanks. When the submarine dives, the tanks are filled with water. When it rises, compressed air is released into the tanks to push out the water. Test this information by making a submarine that is really just one big ballast tank.

You need a plastic bottle with two holes cut in the side (ask an adult to do this), tape, three coins, a piece of plastic tube about 20 in. (50 cm) long, modeling clay, a deep bowl of water.

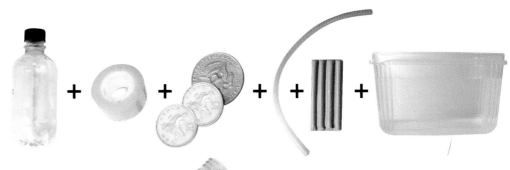

---

1 Tape the coins next to the holes.

2 Put one end of the tube into the neck of the bottle and seal it in place with modeling clay.

3 Place the "submarine" in the water with the coins facing downward. Push it down in the water so that the air escapes and the submarine sinks.

4 Blow down the plastic pipe and **observe** what happens to the water in the submarine and to the submarine itself.

5 Try to make your submarine float just beneath the surface. You may have to pinch the end of the plastic pipe together with your fingers and thumb at some point, to help the air stay in the submarine.

Submarine is filled with water.

Blow into here.

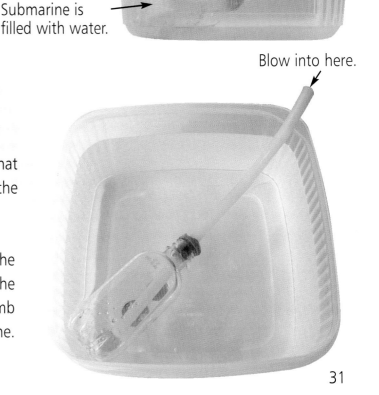

Animals of the Deep

This deep-sea anglerfish is camouflaged so that it is hard to see against the ocean floor. It lies in wait until its prey comes near. Then it wiggles a fleshy tip on its nose to attract the prey and opens its large mouth to catch it.

Near the coasts the water may be only a few feet deep. A little farther out it may be 600 or 1,000 feet (200 or 300 meters) deep. Far out in the oceans the water may be almost 36,000 feet (11,000 meters) deep. Even in the clearest waters, light only penetrates to 3,000 feet (1,000 meters), so much of the deep ocean water is completely dark.

Without light there can be no plant life. Many animals living deep in the oceans rely on food sinking down from the upper waters. This food is the dead remains of other sea creatures. Some animals hunt for prey in the dark water.

Living in dark water

Since there is no light from the Sun, many animals of the deep make their own. They have rows or patterns of spots that give out light when special chemicals made in the animal's body use up energy from the animal's food. The light may shine weakly, so many deep-sea animals have large eyes in order to see it. They use the light to seek out prey and to find partners so that they can breed.

The deep ocean is a vast place and the chances of finding and catching food are small. Many deep-sea fish increase their chances of catching food by having large mouths. The jaws are lined with large numbers of sharp teeth to hold onto any food they catch.

On the ocean floor

Large areas of the ocean floor are covered in mud. The animals that live here have long legs (like the sea spider) or long spines (like sea urchins) to help them move along.

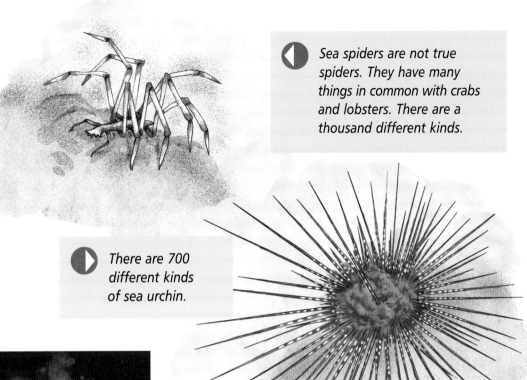

Sea spiders are not true spiders. They have many things in common with crabs and lobsters. There are a thousand different kinds.

There are 700 different kinds of sea urchin.

Hot black water streams upward from a rocky pipe on the ocean floor known as a black smoker.

For many years scientists believed that every living thing on the earth needed energy from the Sun in order to survive. Plants trapped the energy in sunlight and animals fed on the plants to get the energy they needed for life. In 1977 scientists using a **submersible** made an amazing discovery. They found rocky pipes rising 30 feet (10 meters) from the bottom of the ocean. Inside each pipe was an upward stream of hot water coming from a hot spring under the ocean floor. Chemicals in this water had formed the pipes. Other chemicals made the water black and it rose from the pipe tops like smoke rising from chimneys. Scientists found that bacteria were feeding on one of the chemicals in the black water. Worms and crabs were feeding on the bacteria, and these animals were being eaten by fish. All these living things were thriving because of the energy the bacteria took from the chemical —not because of energy from the Sun.

Abandon Ship!

The most dangerous time for people at sea is when a ship sails into a storm. There are openings called hatches between the deck and the rooms below. Normally they are open, so that the crew can move more easily around the ship, but when a storm is coming the hatches are closed. This is called "battening down the hatches," and it stops water from pouring down into the ship and making it more likely to sink.

Even when a ship has closed its hatches, it may be swept onto rocks by a strong current and its **hull** ruptured. Water pours in through the holes, and the crew and passengers prepare to abandon ship.

 These sailors are making their boat ready to sail safely through the storm.

Why a ship sinks

A ship floats because its weight is balanced by its **buoyancy** (see pages 14–15). The weight of a ship consists of the weight of the materials it is built from plus the weight of all the air it contains. When water rushes into a ship, air is pushed out. Water is much heavier than air, so as the ship fills with water its weight becomes greater. Eventually the buoyancy can no longer balance such a large weight and the ship sinks.

Preparing to leave the ship

Ships are equipped with lifeboats and enough life jackets for everyone on board. When a ship has just begun its journey, a lifeboat drill takes place. In this drill everyone is shown how to put on a life jacket and which lifeboat they must go to if they need to abandon ship. This training helps to prevent panic if the ship really has to be abandoned. Panic creates confusion and slows down the quick and orderly filling of the lifeboats.

Into the water

If someone jumps into the water, he or she must swim to keep afloat. Swimming uses up energy and reduces the time a person can survive.

Some people may get their life jacket on, but not be able to reach a lifeboat. They may survive by jumping into the water, since the life jacket will help to keep them afloat. People who cannot even reach a life jacket may survive if they throw an object that floats into the water and then jump in after it. When they come up, they can hold onto the floating object. The life jacket and the floating object allow people to **conserve** their energy, since they do not have to swim, and so they can survive for a longer time in the water. This increases their chances of being rescued.

 At the start of their voyage, passengers on a cruise ship take part in a lifeboat drill.

Dangerous Animals

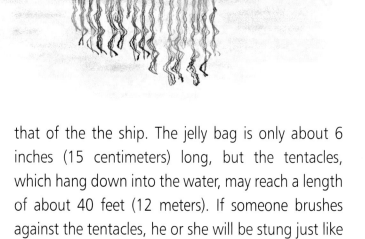

The Portuguese man-of-war cannot swim, but the wind may carry it long distances.

People swimming in the ocean or floating in their life jackets may encounter two main kinds of dangerous animal.

Jellyfish

Most jellyfish have a dome-shaped body and many hanging tentacles. The jellyfish uses the tentacles to catch its prey. On the tentacles are stinging cells. They contain a poison that paralyzes the prey, letting the jellyfish haul it up into its mouth. Some jellyfish, including a type called sea wasps, have such powerful poisons that they can kill people.

The Portuguese man-of-war is an unusual jellyfish. It has a large jelly bag full of gas that helps it float at the water surface. The jellyfish was named after a type of ship, because the bag has a shape similar to that of the the ship. The jelly bag is only about 6 inches (15 centimeters) long, but the tentacles, which hang down into the water, may reach a length of about 40 feet (12 meters). If someone brushes against the tentacles, he or she will be stung just like the man-of-war's prey. The stings are so painful that the person may be unable to continue swimming.

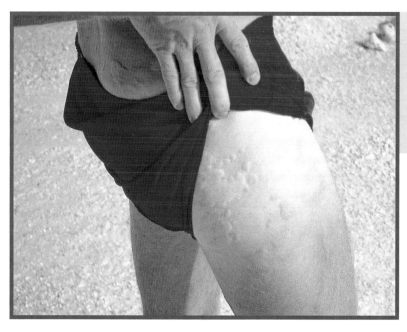

 Usually the result of a jellyfish sting is an itchy or slightly painful rash. Treatment includes applying vinegar and using tape to remove any fragments of tentacle that the jellyfish has left behind.

Sharks

There are many kinds of shark, but the six that have attacked people the most are the bull, nurse, hammerhead, great white, mako, and tiger sharks. The great white is up to 20 feet (6 meters) long.

How to avoid a shark attack
Swim strongly

Sharks are lazy killers. They search for prey that is weak. Many fish swim in groups called schools. If a fish is struggling to keep up with a school or is wounded and swimming erratically, then a shark will detect these movements and attack. Someone swimming in shark-infested waters should make strong movements and keep a regular rhythm. The swimmer should not splash around aimlessly, as this may make sharks think there is a weak or injured animal ready to be eaten.

Keep quiet

Sharks can be attracted by noise, so at times when they are feeding—dawn, dusk, and through the night—keeping quiet should not attract them.

Keep together

If survivors floating in the sea are spread out, they make small targets for a hungry shark. In a group, they make a larger target, which sharks are more likely to leave alone.

Give it a shock

When a shark threatens to attack, people have survived by hitting it on the nose with a stick, slapping the water with their hands, or putting their head underwater and shouting.

Shark repellent

Some life jackets used in tropical waters have a shark repellent on them. Travelers in shark-infested waters may carry shark repellent with them. However, they must use it as a last resort to stop an attack because, once it is used, it spreads out in the water and cannot be used again.

The great white shark is considered the most dangerous of all.

Life Raft

On this ship the inflatable life rafts are stored in metal cylinders above the deck, ready for immediate use if the ship has to be abandoned.

Many ships and boats carry life rafts. A life raft can be packed into a small space so it does not take up much room on board. When it is needed, it can be thrown over the side and inflated. Many life rafts have a **carbon dioxide** cylinder that inflates the **hull** automatically as soon as the raft hits the water.

The hull of the raft is made from one or more **buoyancy** tubes. Each tube is separate so that, if one tube gets punctured, the others do not deflate and the raft can stay afloat. A tube that arches over the hull also fills with gas. This makes a support for the canopy.

The canopy is made from a waterproof material and helps the people on the raft to stay dry. It is also made in a bright color that stands out against the color of the water. This makes it easier for rescue helicopter pilots to see. If a few life rafts are being used, they should be linked together, so that they make a larger colorful object for pilots to spot.

The life raft

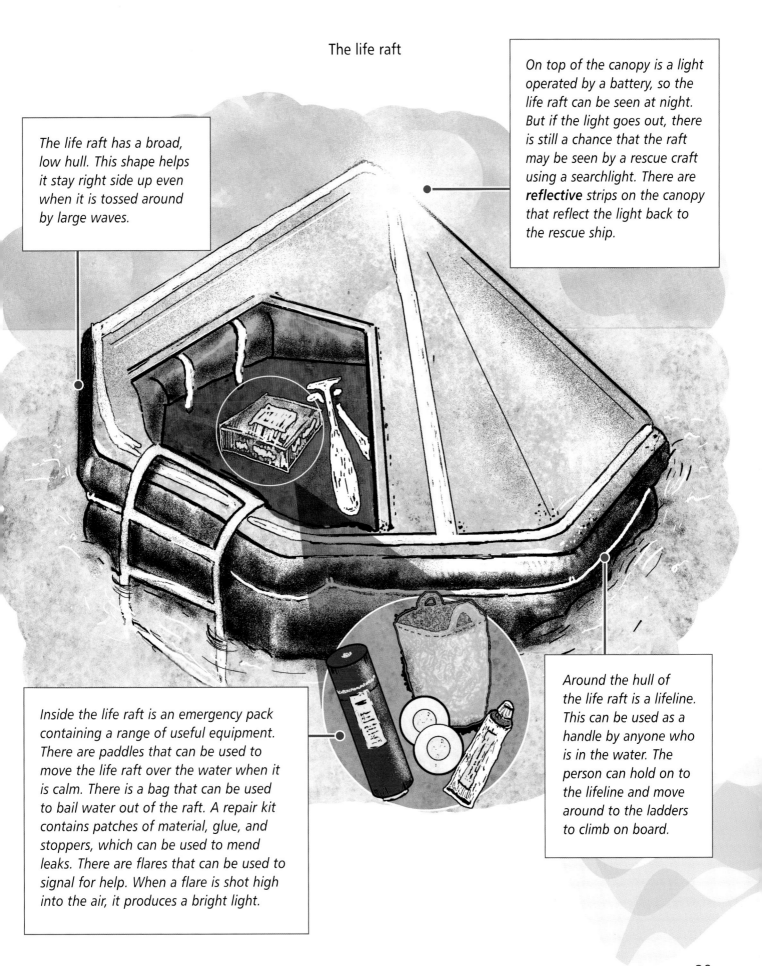

The life raft has a broad, low hull. This shape helps it stay right side up even when it is tossed around by large waves.

On top of the canopy is a light operated by a battery, so the life raft can be seen at night. But if the light goes out, there is still a chance that the raft may be seen by a rescue craft using a searchlight. There are **reflective** strips on the canopy that reflect the light back to the rescue ship.

Inside the life raft is an emergency pack containing a range of useful equipment. There are paddles that can be used to move the life raft over the water when it is calm. There is a bag that can be used to bail water out of the raft. A repair kit contains patches of material, glue, and stoppers, which can be used to mend leaks. There are flares that can be used to signal for help. When a flare is shot high into the air, it produces a bright light.

Around the hull of the life raft is a lifeline. This can be used as a handle by anyone who is in the water. The person can hold on to the lifeline and move around to the ladders to climb on board.

These students at a naval college are taking part in a drill to practice using a life raft.

Keeping healthy in a life raft

Two essentials for life are water and food. You may think that, being surrounded by water, people in a life raft would have plenty to drink—but you would be wrong. Seawater contains large amounts of salt. Although the body needs a certain amount of salt to stay healthy, too much will cause the **kidneys** and other organs to become damaged, which can be lethal. Therefore, water from the ocean must never be drunk.

The emergency kit of many life rafts includes a container of water, but this may not last long. People adrift in a life raft must **conserve** water, just as people do in a desert. They must ration the water so that everyone gets a little each day. They can also collect water when it rains, and when dew forms on the canopy of the raft. The dew can be soaked up with a cloth. This water does not contain salt.

There may be some dry food in an emergency kit, but this must only be eaten when absolutely necessary. The body uses up water when it digests food so, if there is little water on the raft, it is better not to eat.

People on a raft should rest as much as possible. Then they do not use up so much of the energy their body has stored and they will have less need to eat. In hot climates, resting prevents the body from becoming even hotter and sweating heavily. So resting also helps to keep water in the body.

Conserving energy

Your heart pumps blood around your body, carrying food and **oxygen** to all parts of the body. Much of the food and all of the oxygen is used to release energy. When we move, we use a lot of energy and our heart beats fast to supply the **muscles** with their energy needs. In a life raft, you need to conserve energy by moving very little. Use your heartbeat as an indicator of energy use and see how it slows when you rest.

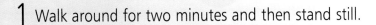

You need a clock and a comfortable place to lie down. **+**

1 Walk around for two minutes and then stand still.

2 Hold out your left hand and turn the palm upward. Put the thumb of your right hand underneath the left hand, so it presses upward on the wrist. Bring the first and second finger of your right hand down onto the wrist and feel for a place where you can feel a throbbing. This is the pulse.

3 Count the number of beats of the pulse in 30 seconds. Double the number of pulse beats you counted to find the number of beats in a minute.

4 Sit still for 5 minutes. Then repeat steps 2 and 3 while sitting. What do you find?

5 Lie down for 5 minutes. Then repeat steps 2 and 3 while lying down.

6 Compare the pulse beats after walking, sitting down, and lying down. What do you find?

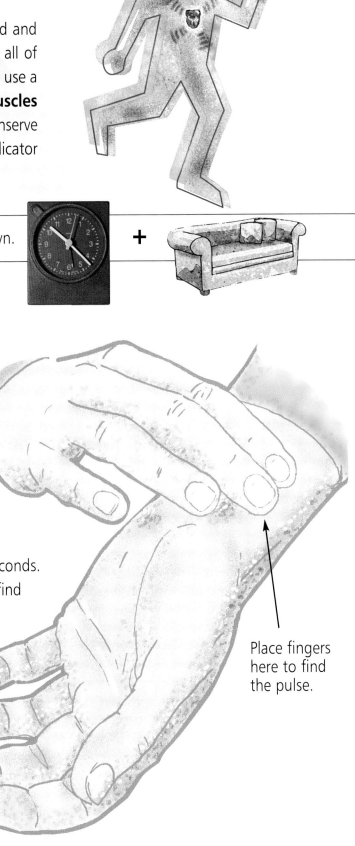

Place fingers here to find the pulse.

Rescue

All ships have a two-way radio to receive and send messages. The messages received come from the coast guard, who work to keep people safe when they visit the shore or pass by in ships. The coast guard radios information to ships about changes in the weather and other ships in the area. The ships radio the coast guard to tell them their position and where they are going.

The radio operator on board a ship that is about to sink calls out "May Day" and repeats it for as long as possible. "May Day" is a signal of distress that is known in all countries. It is really the French phrase "M'aidez!," which means "Help me!"

Rescue services

When the coast guard hears the May Day signal, they try to find where it is coming from and send out a rescue service. This may be a helicopter or a lifeboat or sometimes both. A helicopter crew can get a clear view of the ocean or sea as they fly over it. But a lifeboat crew may not be able to see a life raft if the life raft and the lifeboat are both in **troughs** between very high waves. If this happens, the helicopter can help guide the lifeboat.

Flares

When people in a life raft can hear or see their rescuers approaching, they can attract attention by releasing flares found in the emergency pack. Some flares shoot out smoke. These are used in daylight since the smoke stands out against the

A rescue worker descends a rope hung from the helicopter onto the boat where someone is in trouble.

sky. Other flares, for use at night, shoot out colored light like fireworks. One type of flare, which can be used at any time, has a parachute. When the flare is released it may rise as high as 300 feet (90 meters). Then the parachute opens and the burning flare falls slowly to the sea. This way there is more chance that the flare will be seen.

Testing parachutes

When a flare with a parachute falls through the air, air pushes upward on the parachute with a force called air resistance. If the air resistance is large, the parachute falls slowly. If the air resistance is small, the parachute falls quickly. Compare the air resistance of parachutes by making this test.

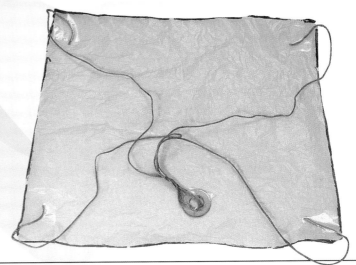

You need a plastic bag cut into different-sized squares, string, tape, two weights such as metal washers.

1 Cut four pieces of string, all the same length.

2 Tape one end of each piece of string to a corner of the smallest piece of plastic.

3 Tape the other ends of the string to a weight.

4 Repeat steps 1–3 to make a parachute from a larger piece of plastic.

5 Drop the two parachutes from the same height and find out which one sinks faster.

6 Repeat steps 1–5 with another pair of parachutes.

7 Switch the parachutes around so that each one has been paired with all the others and figure out which has the greatest air resistance and which has the least.

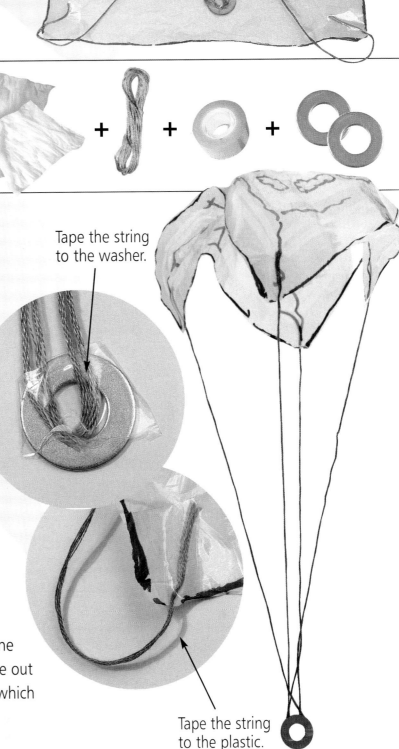

Tape the string to the washer.

Tape the string to the plastic.

All lifeboats are designed for travel in rough weather and carry special safety equipment.

Lifeboat

The kind of lifeboat that is sent out from the coast to rescue people is different from the lifeboats that are lowered from a sinking ship. It is designed to stay afloat in very rough waters.

A ship or boat may sink in a storm because the materials from which it was made split apart where they were joined and water gets in through the split. Sinking may also be caused by water pouring through open hatches into the **hull.** Lifeboats are very well constructed so that they will not break apart in a storm. In addition, whenever a lifeboat takes to the sea, all the hatches are shut. The firmly sealed joints and closed hatches trap air inside the lifeboat and this makes it unsinkable.

The heaviest part of the life boat is its engine. This is placed deep in the hull, where it pushes down strongly on the water. If a wave knocks the lifeboat over, the weight of the engine pushes down on the water again and makes the lifeboat return to its correct position, as the diagrams show.

How a lifeboat stays upright

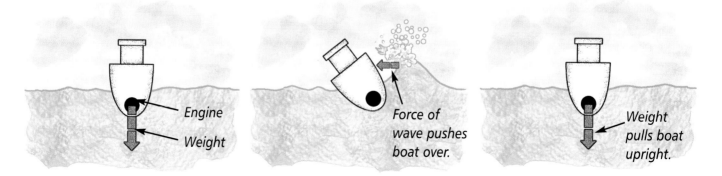

Engine

Weight

Force of wave pushes boat over.

Weight pulls boat upright.

Land ahoy!

Sometimes people adrift after a shipwreck are not spotted by rescuers. They must then watch out for a sign of land and paddle toward it.

● Fluffy clouds called cumulus clouds often form over land, so when these are spotted in a clear sky, land may be in that direction.

● Seabirds usually fly away from land in the morning and back to it in the afternoon. Paddling along the path of the birds may bring a life raft to land. If the sound of birds increases as you paddle, there is a good chance that land is not far away.

● Floating objects such as branches, leaves, or even coconuts could indicate that land is not far away. It may be worth paddling in the direction that these objects seem to be coming from.

● If the color of the ocean or sea changes from blue and green to yellow and brown, there may be the mouth of a river not far away. The change in color is due to particles of mud and rock that have been washed out to sea from the river's mouth.

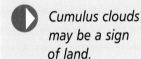

Cumulus clouds may be a sign of land.

The end of the journey

When people reach the end of a journey, they usually feel they have learned a lot along the way. How did you get along, traveling over the oceans? Can you explain how a wave forms and what a black smoker is, or name six dangerous sharks? Along the journey you have also had many chances to try out your science skills of **observing, predicting,** and **experimenting.**

Algae in the oceans produce huge amounts of **oxygen** when they make food in the sunlight. The oxygen passes into the air and travels all over the earth. Wherever you are reading this, you will be breathing in some oxygen that was made in the oceans. So, in a way, you can say that the oceans are helping you to survive at this moment.

Glossary

adapted — having body features that make it easy to survive in certain places

airways — tubes inside an animal that allow air to pass to and from the lungs

algae — tiny plantlike living things that can only be seen clearly with a microscope

baleen — substance in some kinds of whale, that is formed into long flaps in the mouth. Sometimes called whalebone.

ballast — material used to control the way a submarine floats or sinks

buoy — brightly colored floating object, possibly with a light or bell, anchored above underwater hazards to warn boats that they should steer clear

buoyancy — force that pushes upward on any object placed in a liquid

carbon dioxide — gas produced by living things when they use oxygen to release energy from food to keep them alive

cell — tiny structure that is capable of life. Most animals and plants are made from millions of cells.

compressed — squeezed into a small space, such as a tank

conserve — to use something sparingly, so some is saved for use later if needed

crest — highest point of a wave.

diesel — fuel that is changed into vapor and then compressed in an engine to make it explode and power the engine

filter — structure that lets water pass through a fine mesh to separate any small solid particles from it. Some materials filter light, letting through only a small amount of light.

flexible — able to bend a great deal

fluorescent — when something is able to take in light that shines on it and release a glow

foam — mixture of gas and liquid. The gas forms a huge number of bubbles in the liquid, making it appear white and frothy.

gills — part of the body of fish and some other water animals, used for breathing in water

gyre — circular path taken by the currents in most oceans

hull — part of a water craft, such as a ship, that rests in the water

insulation — material that prevents heat or electricity from passing through it.

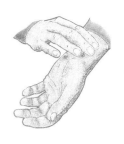

kidney	part of the body that cleans out waste from the blood and lets it leave the body in urine	**sandbar**	pile of sand formed in oceans by the movement of water currents.
lenses	discs of clear glass or plastic that can be used to make light into a beam	**satellite**	object carrying electronic devices such as computers, radio transmitters, and receivers, that moves in a path called an orbit around the earth.
life jacket	jacket made of material that helps keep a body afloat	**spray**	small drops of liquid moving through the air
lung	part of the body that takes in oxygen and releases carbon dioxide	**submersible**	craft that can travel underwater for short periods such as a few hours
mammal	warm-blooded animal that has fur and whose females feed their young milk	**sunblock**	cream that prevents the harmful rays of the Sun from damaging the skin
muscle	part of the body that contracts (gets shorter) and expands (gets larger) to make the body move	**surface tension**	effect made by the way water molecules hold together. The water surface seems as if it has a skin.
observation	looking at the way something is, or the way in which something happens	**swell**	rising and falling of large areas of the sea surface
oxygen	gas found in air and also dissolved in water. It is used by nearly all living things to help keep them alive.	**tide**	movement of the ocean up and down the shore due to the Moon's gravitational pull
pigment	substance that gives color to the body of a living thing	**Tropics**	region between the tropics of Cancer and Capricorn (see pages 6–7)
predator	animal that feeds on other animals	**trough**	low point between two wave crests
reflective	able to reflect light, and therefore easy to see if light shines on it in the dark.	**ultraviolet**	form of energy that travels as waves, with a shorter wavelength than light, and cannot be detected by human eyes

Index